Under the Rocks of the World

Ross Radford

BookLeaf
Publishing

Presentation by *BookLeaf Publishing*

Web: www.bookleafpub.com

E-mail: info@bookleafpub.com

ISBN: 9789395756495

First edition 2022

DEDICATION

My mum and dad, who are always supportive of the work I do and challenges this may bring. Thank you for all your love, support and care, coupled with the filled takeaway boxes of dinners and the clean bags of washing when I come to visit! X

ACKNOWLEDGEMENT

I would like to acknowledge a few people for their support:

The children I have taught and the classes I have shared my poems with. This made me feel more confident to share my poems and write and develop my passion for poetry - thank you!

Miss Haran (my mentor as a trainee teacher), thank you for encouraging me to share my writing with others, and encouraging me to showcase poetry more within our lessons - thank you!

My wonderful Nan, who always spoke with such love and kindness, a lot of what I write is inspired by her and the impact she had on the people within her world.

Thank you to Tony and Sarah for the kind smiles, coffees and putting up with me and my strange ways and work / sleep patterns!

Thank you to my close friends and family, who are always supportive of the things I do and the objectives I set myself however mad they may appear at first - thank you!

Eva, who always inspires me to write, reflect and be myself no matter what. On many of occasions you would be the reason for writing and thinking aloud in such a way that only poetry can provide - thank you (10,000) x

PREFACE

All the poems in this book are an accumulation
of memories, thoughts, feelings and emotions,
some with quite deliberate messages and others
not so much. I have always been reluctant to
share the poems I have written with people, so
this is really the first time I have showcased
some of my writing, which feels particularly
exciting but daunting too. Several of the poems I
have shared with you convey deep meaning and
others are just for fun! There is a real mixture, so
I am sure you will find something that you can
engage with, read depending on your mood and
hopefully enjoy! Good luck!

Under the Rocks of the World

Sometimes the best ones fade into the
background, waiting to be found,
Living under the rocks of the world.

Sometimes the best ones do not make eye
contact at all,
Once you see them, you cannot take your eyes
off of them.
Sometimes the best ones are the quietest and
remain so,
Once they start speaking the room seems to
silence;
For every word you are truly immersed.

Sometimes the best ones are the rarest,
They are unique, special and beautiful in a way
they make very much their own.

Sometimes the best ones cannot be found,
When you grasp the best take an everlasting
hold; do not let go.
Sometimes the best ones surprise you,
Loving in ways they have never loved,
Loving in ways you have never felt love.

Sometimes the best ones possess qualities which seem majestic,
True, pure and innocently perfect.

The best ones are mysteriously uncommon and desperately rare to find,
They are out there under the rocks of the world waiting to feel special again.

Are Ghosts Real Sir?

As the bell rings to start the day, I feel a tug on
my shirt and a child starts to say…

Excuse me sir and I look around, it's little
George four and a half feet from the ground,

It's only gone nine, so I huff, I puff and I sigh,
rolling my eyes and realigning my tie,

What is it George? You're not in your seat, find
your way – pitter pattering feet.

Are ghosts real sir? Not to be scary or cool, it's
just I saw one this morning on my way into
school!

Are ghosts real? Real? What nonsense is this!
Ghosts aren't real! No more candy pop fizz!

It's time for maths, so don't worry about ghosts!
Or I'll have you up here being the timestable
host!!

An hour later, I hear his voice with no doubt.
Are ghosts real? I hear the boy bellow and
shout!

That's it I said, furiously! I'm calling your
mum!! We will then see who has the last bit of
fun!

No, no, please sir! It's really not fair! The ghost
reappeared and he's now sat in your chair!!

I looked with disgust and a face with a frown, I
ran out of class, out of school, out of town!

Just George's big brother, no one remained, the
bed sheet beside him and the grin he had gained!

Clouds of Emotion

The sky is grey and angry like a pack of hungry
wolves.
Winter nights present a sky which seems only to
be filled with sadness.
Cruel, grey fog engulfs the clouds until the sky
is dull and colourless.
Dreary, bleak and unhappy, the cold sky remains
dark and stern.

The sky is cloudy and light like white, fluffy
marshmallows.
Clouds bound amongst the sky in such effortless
ways like they are floating with happiness.
Delicate, transparent winds whistle gently over,
under and between the soft edges of the clouds.
The wind elegantly dances through the sky
tiptoeing confidently and bold.

The sky is turquoise and calm like a still, open
ocean.
The summer sky is warm and untroubled sitting
delicately undisturbed.
Bright, glistening sunshine beams through the
clear, tranquil sky.

The beautiful, unblemished sky peers down with a cheeky, radiant smile.

6

When I Think of You

When I think of you, my dimples smile
intertwined within the smile itself.
Cheek to cheek, the corners of my mouth turn in,
Soft sculpted edges that can only be seen whilst
I think of you,
Thinking so proudly of my special person.

When I think of you I go somewhere -
Somewhere where the entrance door reads,
'contentment'.
It is far away from here, a place that seems to
deny the most ordinary of things-
Gravity is merely a myth.
This place is a bubble of all things good,
It is light, effortless and when I think of you it is
freedom.
You cannot navigate here, but when you finally
know, you have it.
You are there.

When I think of you, I ponder and pine,
When I think of you I affirm all those milestones
which only seem possible with you, next to you
and by your side.

When I think of you, I value every moment you
are mine and I yours,
I ponder, I wonder, when I think of you.

When I think of you, I feel imperfectly perfect,
For man said they would come in twos and you
are mine and I am yours.
I felt like a winter's scarf tossed in the wind,
A snow globe shaken and thrown,
Then the wind stopped and the snow settled.
Nothing before you was wrong, only everything
after you is right,
Smiles become our reality.

When I think of you, I dream, I actualize and I
live within that entrance door.
Every step, be it a trainer or a croc is aligned
with yours, holding your little hand by your side.

For I love you and the thoughts that emerge
from you just being you.
My poem to you | 10,000

Mums

Mums. They are amazing and inspirational, they
like to see you happy,
From birth they are with you and regularly
change your nappy.
She is wonderful and she is special in ways no
one will truly know,
She is your personal cheerleader and the loudest
at your show!

Mums. They are smiley, they are proud, they
sing it from the roof tops,
Looking after you when you're sick and buying
medicine from the shops!
She is hardworking and resilient, there's not
much more for her to do,
She will call the doctors and run you there when
you are poorly with the flu.

Mums. They are tremendous, they are perfect,
they celebrate your wins,
They'll shower you with kisses from head to
cheek to chin!
She is one of a kind and selfless, she'd give you
the clothes off her back,
She always does all she can to keep you right on
track!

Mums. Their love for you is sacred, it's as strong
as you and me,
A mum's love is eternal and fills the heart with
glee.
She is warm and she is loving, she is someone
who cannot be replaced,
Mother, mummy, mamma, it brings a smile to
her face!

You are truly blessed to have the best so tell her
when you can,
30 or older no excuses, you could shout it from
your van!
She is accepting, she is bubbly, she is beautiful
inside out,
Motherly, maternal and mindful, there'll never
be a drought.

What more can you say, actually the list could
go on and on,
It's happily ever after, starting with once upon…
Thank you for being my mum, for being the
very best,
Thank you for being mine, I know I'm truly
blessed!

My poem to my wonderful Mum!

Timely Memories

Faded memories rejuvenate, dance and sing, and present themselves on a blank canvas like early motion pictures.

The lavender drawstring bags that were placed under our pillowcases still smell as fragrant and calming as they did then.

The boutique glass jar filled with dolly mix was always brimming with bright, wonderful colours as it sat above the dormant fireplace.

The inside of cupboard, through the lounge, recorded our heights as we grew, each year lined with a new pencil mark: Ellis, Ross, Charlie…

The close was filled with the sounds of joyful children, the echo of ball games, the vans of dads and grandads and occasionally the ice cream mans too.

Demanding days showered with the sounds of their west island white terrier and border collie always brought an ironic sense of tranquility to our visits.

The green was just a stone's throw away,
although then it felt like an expedition, past the
church and around the corner, the prestigious
green gazed at us all seasons of the year.

Standing largely and bold, combing his hair
backwards, left then right and over again. He
applied copious amounts of brylcream whilst
bouncing his red, plastic comb over and over
through his silky, styled hair.

He would take us to pick conkers from the local
horse chestnut trees, drill the holes, wrap the
string and play us to win.

His voice was calm, peaceful and quite effortless
through the harmonies of 'Stand by Me' and
'Wonderful World', singing sporadically as he
travelled from room to room.

'Home & Away' was where hot, home cooked
dinners would begin, sitting patiently hoping this
was followed by her famous and tasty semolina
and jam 'pudding'; only she could make it so
delightful and moreish.

Beautiful, kind-hearted, a superlative in all
forms, quite literally king and queen of the

close. What if time could rejuvenate, what to
give one more day or two at most!

Pets, Pets, Pets!

Loud and obnoxious or fluffy and cute,
Food pouches, biscuits, raw meat or fruit?
Pets are wonderful, it's great knowing their
yours!
Big, small, fat or thin, beaks, tails or paws.

They smile with their eyes, whiskers or beaks,
Staring right at you, it's as if they can speak.
When you are down and missing your glow,
They come to your company as if they might
know.

Sitting in your lap, beside you or perched,
Waiting and waiting, while you research.
Working hard, they resiliently sit by,
Yawning and stretching, a cry and sigh.

We love our brilliant pets and they love us back
too,
Clean water and food, make sure you do.
A healthy home, walks, snuggles and care,
Look after them dearly, one, ten or a pair!

The People of Your World

It is how you enter the world, from their love,
these are the people in your life who treasure
you.
These people, your guardian angels, announce
themselves as mums, dads, carers, guardians and
grandparents.
They help you find your feet from birth, your
first steps in a frightening and ever changing
world, and metaphorically hereafter.
These are the people who care, love and support
you in your life.
In every victory, success and triumph; tuning in
no matter what the weather may forecast.

They smile for you when you wonder what the
day may bring,
They see through the stains of doubt and the
fluctuating negativity.
They are the most resilient of torch lights in a
colourless, empty room.

In the depths of sorrow, they are the arm that
brings you towards peace.

In the whirlwinds of concern, they are the
moment of realization that brings to back to
familiarity.
In the hustle of hatred, they are the people who
stand tall and proud, directing you into the
current of hope.

It is how you enter the world, from their love,
these are the people in your life who care for
you.
These people, your guardian angels, announce
themselves as mums, dads, carers, guardians and
grandparents.
They help you find your feet from birth, your
first steps in a frightening and ever changing
world, and metaphorically hereafter.
They lead the way when the path is blind and the
shadows seem only to fall on your face.
In the bleakest of times, they are the people
whose smiles remind you it is only a page within
your storybook.

They send you melodies in the sound of silence,
They free your mind when words circle you with
chaos.
They harmonize with you when you are
engulfed in doubt,
They abolish the entrapment when you are but a
castaway in a sombre night.

It is how you enter the world, from their love,
these are the people in your life who love you.
They replace your doubt with hope, hate with
love and your emptiness with contentment.
These people love you with no contracts or
conditions, they love you endlessly for you are
their world.

Dads

Dads.

Every tool, every solution, he always comes to the rescue - it's dad!
One in a million, entertaining and caring - I might add.

He drives you to school, parties and even your friends,
He collects you after dark 8, 9 and even past 10!
Rain or shine he'll greet you with a smile,
Helpful always, never sometimes or in a while.
Rescuing away, day by day, and even by night,
He's super my dad, my hero, my knight!

Every tool, every solution, he always comes to the rescue - it's dad!
One in a million, lovable and playful - I might add.

Not the loudest of dads, but with phrases from his heart,
It's how he shows his love and this is just the start.

Don't worry, and leave it to me,
Or just one moment, let me go and see!
No problem too big and no problem to small,
From DIY to hugs, my dad does it all!

Selfless, kind, the most caring of men,
Can you pick me up? Yes, I'll see you just then!

My poem to you, Dad!

Sensational Lights

Fireworks glitter, shimmering and loud,
Fireworks red-blue-green and proud.
Bang, fizz, whirl and pop,
Fireworks - they just won't stop!
Fireworks spiralling, whooshing and screech,
Children please, keep out of reach!

Fireworks explosive, dramatic and bright,
Frightening fast, watch them ignite!
Bang, fizz, whirl and pop,
Fireworks - they just won't stop!
The gurgle, the hiss, the cloud of smoke,
Playing with fireworks is no joke!

Guy Fawkes, gun powder and ammunition,
Fireworks starting, get in position!
New Year's Eve or Halloween,
Ramadan or parties between.
Stand back it's time to ignite,
Fireworks appearing high in flight!
Fireworks dancing and singing aloud,
Fireworks over, dispersing crowd!

Please Can I Be a Pirate Daddy?

I wish I could be a pirate Daddy, oh please, oh
please, oh please,
But what if I'm no good, Daddy? I don't like the
hard storm seas!
Are you sure it's a pirate you want to be, choose
something we both agree?
But I wish I could be a pirate Daddy and
triumph treasures with ease!

I wish I could be a pirate Daddy, oh please, oh
please, oh please,
But what if I'm no good, Daddy? I don't like the
ocean breeze!
Are you sure it's a pirate you want to be,
fingernails full of grease?
But I wish I could be a pirate Daddy not the
princess with the peas!

I wish I could be a pirate Daddy, oh please, oh
please, oh please,
But what if I'm no good, Daddy? I don't like the
cold wind freeze!
Are you sure it's a pirate you want to be, no pink
warm cosy fleece?

But I wish I could be a pirate Daddy, sailing the seven seas!

I wish I could be a pirate Daddy, oh please, oh please, oh please,
But what if I'm no good, Daddy? I don't like to be called a he's!
Are you sure it's a pirate you want to be, I'll have to take away your key?
Fine! I'll stay at home till tomorrow playing in the house top tree!!!

Twins

Twins, twins, twins!
Wow, you look the same! Are you really twins?
Yes, yes, yes, although there's one who always
sins!
Twins that must be cool, that must be fun, what's
it like?
Known no different, it was harder riding my
bike!
So, you must be identical? You are both exactly
the same!
No, no, no! We are different! Starting with our
names!
We are separate! Individuals! We merely share
the same DNA.
So enjoy us as our own person, that's all I wish
to say!

I Love You, I Do, I Do

I love you, I love you, I do, I do.
I do love you deeply, you don't understand,
Let me try and show you, take hold of my hand.
No words big, strong or great enough to express
or convey my feelings,
But I'll show you every day, my love for you
and its meaning.

You are my last thought before bed, and first in
the morning,
The way I see you through these lenses, I'm
certainly adoring.
It's not a phase, lust or a moment, it's permanent
to me,
Explaining what you mean to me, requires the
word count of a degree!

I thought I loved you when we met, certainly by
the fourth or fifth date,
But every day I love you more, so maybe it's
just our fate?
I really feel so lucky, to have such a beautiful
best friend,
Trying to convey these feelings, so one day
you'll comprehend.

You're kind, caring and special, I'll tell you till
I'm blue,
My love for you is innumerable, and now it's
you and me as two.
I can't wait to spend my life with you, for we
seemed to pick each other,
I hope this explains what I couldn't, my perfect,
little lover!
I love you, I love you, I do, I do.

Life as a Trainee Teacher

She wasn't a Jessica or a Sharon, although she went by the name of Year 2's Miss Haran.

To begin she was unsure, fiery and red, she would look at him with such dread; smiling, only 10 weeks to go, she said…

Week 1: Sometimes a good morning but lots of meetings, although lack of friendly greetings, and he needs to work on Teacher Standard part 2, only 9 weeks to go she said, oh phew!!

Week 2: Frosty, slightly cold if truth be told. The mentor thought this student is rather bold, but she mentored away. There might have been a slight smile by the end of the day… only 8 weeks to go she thought, and she smiled and continued with the teaching and taught.

Week 3: The few and far good mornings began to fade, she was pleased with the progress her student had made, or perhaps just the perfect cup of tea served to her chair upon her knee. Regardless, 7 weeks to go she thought, and she smiled away as before and continued with the teaching and taught.

Week 4: Cups of tea and cheeks quite rosy, she still wasn't sure as this pretty boy was posy? Yet she exchanged a joke, a laugh and a smile, and was happier for a while. 6 weeks to go and the final date approaching, be sensible she told him, can't be no more coasting!

Week 5: She was hard at work with observations and obligations, teaching away day by day. 31 students, the big kid and the 30 little ones too. The place was nice, she laughed a lot, if she didn't she'd lose the plot! 5 weeks to go, her voice tone was changing, the student took note as this is what his external mentor had spoke.

Week 6: Time was flying now and the days felt like disco balls, he was teaching and learning and not quite so many falls. Strange to say, 4 weeks to go and yet no smile this time, who would know…

Week 7: The mentor was marvellous, brilliant, just great, but the placement end was looming he could see the date! He had learnt a lot and was extremely thankful, although unqualified teachers need a tankful! 2 weeks left, that didn't make him feel the best! The days just spiralled off as the end was in sight, 2 then 1, then it's finished, right?!

Week 8: The external mentor came to visit and was extremely happy- the ending was near, the student and children could shed a tear. He had learnt loads and the mentor had taught him well, the impact he'd made, so good, maybe a spell?

Week 9: Last week to go, it's finally here! No more story maps, sticks and dots, or other manipulatives too, the student had learnt a lot and here's his thank you! My teaching journey is on its way, so really just two things left to say… goodbye and thank you!

The Boys Who Loved Sweets

Two naughty boys in the shop giving their poor
mum grief,
Sulking, trudging and tears rolling onto the
floor!
We want sweets! No, no, no, they just rot your
teeth!
The boys punch and kick the air! But Mum, we
want more!
Sweets, sweets, sweets!!! The makers of
mischief gave no relief!
Poor mum, gripped her hair and shouted, I can't
take anymore!
For a moment the boys paused, wide-eyed in
disbelief!
Sorry how we acted mum, we were naughty, just
wrong before.
But we do want sweets one said! Red-faced, she
could not believe!

Everyone Gets Sick

It's always hard to see a loved one in discomfort,
To see them uncomfortable,
To see them readjusting, huffing and sighing,
alternating from and into every position to try
and feel some relief.
Remember, everyone gets sick.

It's always hard to see a loved one get poorly,
To see them feeling under the weather,
To see them curled up in a ball in the middle of
the day watching every minute drag on longer
than the last.
Remember, everyone gets sick.

It's always hard to see a loved one in pain.
To see them toss and turn all hours of the night,
To see them squint, squirm and wrinkle their
nose in pain waiting for that miracle that may
never come.
Remember, everyone gets sick.

It's always that bit easier when you have
somebody to talk to,
When you have somebody to care for you,

When you have somebody to do the things you
can't.
Remember, everyone gets sick.

It's always that bit easier when you have
somebody who can make your day more
bearable,
When you have somebody that makes you feel
hopeful,
When you have somebody to show you love in
the greatest of ways at the most uncomfortable
and difficult of times.
Remember, everyone gets sick.

Caribbean Me

Mi woke in de morning from dat glimmering
sun,
De weather looks bright, but no time for fun!
Mi lay in mi hammock, swinging to not fro,
Combing my hair, look – de best afro!
De ocean is close, hear it swosh and swish,
Don't look now, it's a JELLLLY FISHHHH!

Cold mornin' water surrounds sandy beach,
Soon enough warm, dat now out of reach!
Mi lay in mi hammock, swinging to not fro,
Combing mi hair, look – de best afro!
Mi name is Samson, Samson de great,
One more ting, irie - relate?

De ocean is waving, shall mi wave it back?
Mi father drinks de rum from de top of de rack!
Mi lay in mi hammock, swinging to not fro,
Combing mi hair, look – de best afro!
An explosion of sound, it is de steel drum,
I play de chorus wid just dis thumb.

De trees clap and dance from de roots to de
beach,
Too faas up, mi say it and preach!

Mi lay in de hammock, swinging to not fro,
Combing mi hair, look – de best afro!
De weather is glorious, holla nice and loud,
Loud as a trumpet in de Kingston Town crowd!

Jamaica a beauty, it de yard for mi,
Linstead Market, plenty ackee.
Mi lay in de hammock, swinging to not fro,
Combing my hair, look – de best afro!
Pickney dem say, mi respond wid mi?
Of course it yuh, who else it be?

Back to School!

My books are crammed and my bag is full,
A good day today! I will break no rule!
Rucksacks ready, pupils glide,
No homework again, where shall I hide?

Through the damp door and curious corridor,
Today's a good day? I'll show Miss More!
Playtime has arrived, whooshing and screech,
The ball on the roof, (sigh) and out of reach!
I chase my friends as fast a lightning bolt;
As fierce as a lion, Mr. Brown screams halt!
Rucksacks ready, pupils glide;
No homework again, where shall I hide?

The bell dances, shakes and waves,
Playtime is over, stop the rave!
Time for maths, I hate this lesson,
One thing worse, grammar sessions!
Dienes, rulers, pencil pots,
Place value charts and table spots!
Rucksacks ready, pupils glide,
No homework again, where shall I hide?

Not long left, my brain is ticking,
Lunchtime hurry, please not sickening!!

Rucksacks ready, pupils glide;
No homework again, where shall I hide?!?!

Motionless Miles

As I write, standing here, ants begin to run across my page confused and directionless pressing their feelers into each line on the paper as if they are creating their own pathways.

For miles there is a stillness and occasional breeze. The tall, hard strands of deeply rooted wheat are untouched and motionless, although they seem to hang their head in defeat as the hot, powerful sun beams down permanently onto them.
The road leading to the nearby farm widens, narrows, then widens again once more, but is left hazy as clouds of dust litter the air and then slowly begin to settle from the framer's tractor moving across the firm earth. Distant aeroplanes glide through the sky loudly blowing hot air through the spinning propellers; the sound is familiar yet out of place.

The sun sits in the background of the clouds like a ball of fire; it shines brightly dazzling my eyes with a fierce, beaming sparkle. Its sunlight is golden yellow and relentless. The surrounding

trees and leaves seem to pray for shade, or even
rain.

There are small, thin grasshoppers singing in
groups like rehearsing classical musicians
calling for one another to play in intervals. The
meandering, age-stained fence collapses against
the strong thick roots in a semi-circle that
follows the trunk of the tree. The rest of the trees
seem to watch over, leaning against one another
like big brothers gazing out across the horizon,
as I do now.

The colours of green, brown and yellow mingle
like droplets of water forming a sea of autumnal
colour. In the distance, the squawk of the swans
echo and a strong ear can make out powerful
wings as they circle the neighbouring ponds.
While I write, every so often there is an
occasional car or humming engine from the next
adjoining road before the final turn in the
opposite direction, taking him or her further
away.

The slight, mild breeze has become more
obvious as the sun begins to settle and the air
around me gently vibrates through my shirt,
across my sleeves and up. The brief but
refreshing coolness is welcomed as it meets my
warm neck for the first time.

Unprovoked Beauty

The beautiful ocean claps against the rocks as the wind picks up.

There is a stream of glimmering light where seawater meets golden sand for the very first time.

White, salty foam like a shoal of mini sponges emerges to the surface.

Sand is dragged and thrown forwards and backwards as the water crashes between the waves.

The ocean seems to be fuelled with hatred and anger, lashing out with each breaking wave.

Like a high, wide cocoon collapsing in on itself, the waves unravel and loosen still surging inwards.

Faster, stronger and more volatile, each wave more destructive than the last.

Like a possessed demon from the depths of hell,
its surges once more with an almighty power.

Each strike crashes onto the beach as it builds up
for a final blow.

With an unhinged glare, the sea prepares… one -
final - time.

Dancing its last dance, it leaves an everlasting
impression and devastating reminder...

It is beautiful thing in its calm, unprovoked
form.